Gerald L or Darleen J Klevene
2421 - 88th St S
Wisconsin Rapids WI 54494

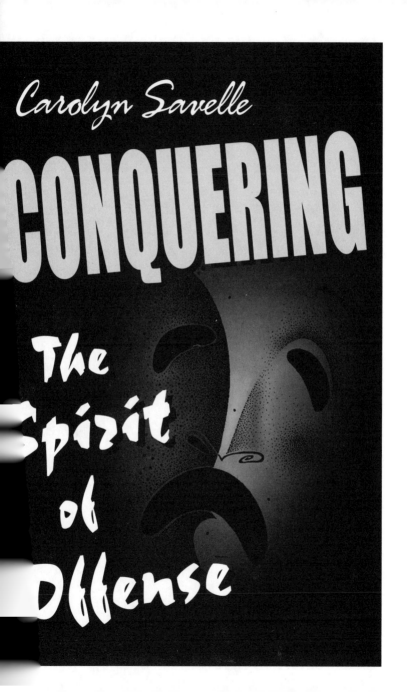

Carolyn Savelle

CONQUERING

The Spirit of Offense

CONQUERING
THE SPIRIT OF OFFENSE

by Carolyn Savelle

CONQUERING THE SPIRIT OF OFFENSE

ISBN 0-9655352-1-5
Unless otherwise stated, all scripture
quotations are taken from
The King James Version of the Bible.

Jerry Savelle Publications
P.O. Box 748
Crowley, TX 76036
817/297-3155

TABLE OF CONTENTS

CHAPTER

I

Offenses: Satan's Trap

I think I'm safe in saying that we have all had our feelings hurt at one time or another. We've all felt insulted by someone or felt like an injustice was done to us. Usually, when our feelings are hurt by someone, instead of letting it go, resentment begins to build on the inside of us. In this book, I want to share with you what kind of dramatic impact resentment, bitterness, unforgiveness and offenses can have in your life if they are not dealt with and uprooted. They can literally stop you from ever achieving success. You'll also learn how to confront the offense, how to release it and how to move on to the next level with God in your life.

Once you realize how devastating an offense is in your heart, you'll want to quickly dig it out and be free once and for all. I began doing this study on offenses simply because the Lord was showing me that I had been offended, and it was time to forgive so I could move on. I am no different than anyone else. The opportunity to be offended affects me too. But I've learned the key to conquering the spirit of offense, and I want to share it with you.

Have you ever been around someone who constantly talks about their past and how badly they were hurt? Perhaps they were in an abusive relationship, or grew up in an abusive family and have never been able to forgive the person who abused them. Whether the offense entered them due to abuse or whether they've been offended simply over a comment someone made about them, they must let it go.

If you have been abused mentally, physically or even sexually, you need to ask the Holy

Spirit to come on the scene and help you release the offense in your life that has caused you so much pain. The anointing destroys the yoke of bondage - all types of bondages - even the bondage of being offended. Jesus is there to comfort you, and to help you get over this hurt in your life.

> *Who is weak, and I am not weak?*
> *who is offended, and I burn not?*
>
> 2 Corinthians 11:29

> *Who is weak, and I do not feel*
> *[his] weakness? Who is made to*
> *stumble and fall and have his*
> *faith hurt, and I am not on fire*
> *[with sorrow or indignation]?*
>
> 2 Corinthians 11:29
> *The Amplified Bible*

We can clearly read in this scripture that Jesus is right with us, and He is willing and able to help us through the hard times in our lives. There are many, many avenues in which one can be offended. The spirit of offense can affect us on a daily basis. We have to choose to not let people, words, or actions offend us.

A number of years ago, there was a prominent minister in the land who made a statement that really upset me. He said that he felt like the five-fold ministry office of the Teacher was over with. He went on to say that it was only the day of the Prophet and the day of the Pastor. The other three offices (out of the five) were done away with. He even said, "I think Jerry Savelle is one of the greatest teachers there is in the Body of Christ but the day of the Teacher is over with."

I became so offended at that statement - defending my husband. He is a teacher. I thought to myself, "What does he want us to do? Bring out all the teachers, line them up and have a firing squad used on them because we don't need them anymore?"

I became so offended at this man that any time I would see him on the television, I would turn the TV off immediately. I became critical of the things that he said and did. I walked around with the spirit of offense in my heart, totally unaware of it. I was completely unaware that I had fallen into the pit that Satan had dug for me. I thought I was protecting my husband, instead I was hurting myself.

When I began to realize what had happened to me (that I had become offended), I had to repent. I had to get on my knees and ask God to forgive me. It wasn't until I began doing this study on offense, that I realized just how detrimental holding an offense is to one's life. I did not realize that allowing unforgiveness to stay in my heart could stop my growth in Christ.

I was offended at that man. But I had to purposely make a decision to release all unforgiveness, hurt feelings and offense toward that man once and for all. Then I began to pray for him. When you sincerely pray for someone, you can't be critical of them. Prayer will cause you to fall in love with that person. I wanted to be like David in the Bible and walk around with a loving heart, a forgiving heart, letting God be judge and not raising my voice against God's anointed.

Offense: A Sign of the End Time

If you'll notice in Matthew 24, the disciples asked Jesus as He was departing the temple area one morning, "What will be the signs of Your coming and of the end of the world?" And Jesus' reply to the disciples was:

> *..And then shall many be offended, and shall betray one another, and shall hate one another. And many false prophets*

*shall rise, and shall deceive many.
And because iniquity shall
abound, the love of many shall
wax cold. But he that shall endure
unto the end, the same shall be
saved.*
Matthew 24:10-13

The Amplified Bible says,

*And then many will be offended
and repelled and will begin to
distrust and desert [Him Whom
they ought to trust and obey] and
will stumble and fall away, and
betray one another and pursue
one another with hatred.*

Matthew 24:10

Notice the sign of the end time: ***Many*** will
be offended. We have never, in any generation,
seen so many people taking people to court, and
suing one another over the pettiest things.

The *"love of many growing cold"* in that verse in the context of what was being spoken about there, is referring to people who had the *agape* love of God in their heart at one time. So it's the Christians whose love has grown cold. The many who at one time wouldn't think of taking one another to court or suing one another have turned cold. For example, I recently read an article in a newspaper about a man suing a sunscreen company because he was sunburned while on vacation. Can you believe that? People are suing one another over ridiculous issues.

I want us to look at the word *offense.* In Grosset Webster's Dictionary, the word *offense* is defined as "resentment, an affront, an injustice, a misdemeanor, attack, or aggressive." Webster's New World Dictionary defines *offense* or *to offend* as "to commit a sin or a crime, to create resentment, anger, to hurt the feelings of or to be insulted." As I mentioned earlier, I'm sure we've all had our feelings hurt in our life time. An offense is simply Satan's trap designed to hold you back from ever being all that God has called you to be. Notice what Luke says about offenses:

> *Then said he unto the disciples, It is impossible but that offences will come: but woe unto him, through whom they come!*
>
> Luke 17:1

The Amplified Bible says,

> *And [Jesus] said to His disciples, Temptations (snares, traps set to entice to sin) are sure to come, but woe to him by or through whom they come!*

It says it is impossible but that offenses will come. Snares, traps set to entice one to sin are sure to come. So knowing that the opportunity to become offended will come, we need to learn what to do when it comes our way.

Jesus was saying to watch out or take heed because they are going to come. Things will come across your life like bait to a trap, and if you take that bait, then you're going to fall into the pit that Satan has set for you. We have to be so smart that we don't fall for offenses, that we don't fall for these traps and snares that have been set by Satan to capture us and cause us to never reach the potential that God fully intends for us to reach.

The Greek word for *offense* is **skandalon.** We get our English word *scandalize* from it. It means "the bait of a trap." The word originally referred to the part of the trap to which the bait was attached to entrap or ensnare the animal. That's what an offense is in our lives. It is the bait that Satan sets to ensnare us or entrap us to get us to fall into the pit that he has dug for us.

When I was a young girl, my grandfather would take all the grandchildren into the forest with him, and he would teach us how to trap. It was so exciting as a young child to be able to carry those traps over my shoulder and go out into the woods with him, watch him bait the trap and then camouflage it so that the animal would unknowingly be caught.

It sounds horrible now, but it was so much fun as a little girl to get to go with my Grandpa out into the woods to see what we had caught through the night and be able to carry our bounty back home. I can't imagine me doing that now, but as a little girl, it was exciting.

The key was to keep the traps camouflaged in order to capture the animal. That's exactly what Satan endeavors to do where you and I are concerned so we do not see how detrimental holding offense in our hearts is to our lives and to our Christian walk. If we fall for the bait of offense, then we've been ensnared, and he has taken us captive at his will.

Haven't you heard the phrase, "They owe me," or "He's going to pay for this"? Jesus could have had that attitude toward us, but He didn't. He chose to forgive us; therefore, we must forgive those who have hurt us.

> *And then shall many be offended, and shall betray one another, and shall hate one another.*

> Matthew 24:10

When you become offended, then unforgiveness comes in and then hatred sets in.

> *THIS KNOW also, that in the last days perilous times shall come. Having a form of godliness but denying the power thereof: from such turn away.*

> 2 Timothy 3:1,5

We see unforgiveness is running rampant in the land today. Unforgiveness comes as a result of an offense. First, offense has to occur, then unforgiveness which eventually turns into hatred.

> *And herein do I exercise myself, to have always a conscience void of offence toward God, and toward men.*
>
> Acts 24:16

Most people don't like exercise, especially when they first start out. It hurts too bad. But after a period of time, if you consistently do it over and over, then you begin to enjoy working out and feeling better about yourself. Anything you do for 21 days consistently becomes a habit.

Paul is saying in this verse that we have to work at not being offended. It takes effort to stay free of offense, but it can be done.

> *When angry, do not sin; do not ever let your wrath (your exasperation, your fury or indignation) last until the sun goes down. Leave no [such] room or foothold for the devil, [give no opportunity to him].*
>
> Ephesians 4:26
> *The Amplified Bible*

This is a familiar verse, but it's time we realize the seriousness of it. It's so vital that we get all offenses out of us now. We've got to get free of them. Please notice that God even sets a time limit on how long we can remain angry. We are not to even go to bed until we have it settled.

Offended at Others' Blessings

I want to share an example from the Bible of someone being offended and what it ended up costing them. In Genesis 4, we read of a story that is familiar to every one of us, the story of Cain and Able. This is where an offense took place. Remember how Able brought a blood sacrifice by faith to God and God had respect for his offering? Cain, on the other hand, brought the first fruits, the best fruits of his own efforts which was not what God had instructed him to do.

They had been taught by their parents the way they should approach God was by blood sacrifice. But Cain wanted to approach God his own way. He was not ignorant of the proper way to approach God. It had to be by blood sacrifice. Isn't that just like religion today? They want to approach God their own way, not the way that God has instituted and set up in His Word.

> *But unto Cain and to his offering he had not respect.*
>
> **Genesis 4:5**

Why? Because it was not a blood sacrifice.

But Cain was very angry and offended and the Word says *his countenance fell.* Cain, by his own flesh and by his own will (not doing as his parents had instructed him), felt rejected. He thought that all of his hard work and his best efforts were not appreciated. He became offended at God because he didn't feel like God appreciated what he had done.

We have the same thing going on in the church today. The same feeling of not being appreciated. "Doesn't the Pastor know how hard I work around here? Don't they know how much I sacrifice, how much time I give up coming down here, working in the nursery, working in the children's church, working in Sunday School? Don't they know how much private time I give up in preparation for this?"

We have that same spirit in the Church, in the home, and in the workplace today - feeling like our efforts aren't appreciated. "Doesn't anyone see the hours I work?"

We have to be so careful, when we begin to have thoughts like that. It implies that you've been offended at some point. You have to continually put a guard and a watch over thoughts like this. Have you ever said, "I work around here and no one ever says thank you!! No one ever pats me on the back"? You've been offended.

You can become offended when you see others being blessed or appreciated. When you feel like you should be receiving the praise or the promotion, but others are — you can be offended.

You could have the thought, "Well, I know I give as much as they do, in fact I give more! I tithe. I give. I sow. I'm always giving. Why are they being blessed and getting a new car when I've been standing in faith and believing for the new car?"

You have to become so careful that you don't allow those thoughts to come into your mind because at some point you'll become offended. We have to get the spirit of offense out of our heart and out of our mind and not fall into that trap that Satan has set up for us.

Offended At God

Looking at the life of Moses, you'll remember God sent Moses to deliver the children of Israel, to set them free and bring them out of the bondage of Egypt and into the promised land. You know the story how he sent out the twelve spies and there were ten that came back with a bad report and two that came back with a good report. And all the congregation of people began to murmur and complain.

If you go back and read that in context, they were offended at God. They said to Moses, "Why have you brought us out here to die?" Because they were offended at God, and they were offended at Moses, that generation never saw the land of promise. (Numbers 14:1-45)

I think that illustration reveals to us that if we become offended at God or anyone else, we'll never see our land of promise. We will never see what God has fully promised us, and we'll be continually held back from God's best for our lives.

We have to be a man or woman with a heart towards God who will forgive any offense that's been committed unto us. We cannot continue to harbor offense and unforgiveness in our heart. It doesn't matter what people say about you, or what people do against you. You cannot harbor offenses in your heart.

How many Christians do you know today who are offended at God? Possibly because they think God didn't come through for them. I know people who are offended at God because they had a loved one who was sick and wasn't healed of that sickness, and they became offended at God. They felt like God didn't hear their prayer. Or perhaps a loved one died, and they feel like God didn't answer their prayer, so the spirit of offense enters towards God.

There are a lot of variables in a situation like that, and we have to realize that it's not God's fault because maybe a particular prayer wasn't answered the way we felt it should have been answered. **You cannot get offended at God.**

There was a time in David's life when he became offended at God. He had to go out and pray, seek God and go before Him over a period of three months before he realized that it was he who had the problem and not God (2 Samuel 6:6-12). Well, let me save you the time and let you know right now: if you have offense in your heart towards God, it's not God's fault. It's you who needs to get that offense out immediately!

CHAPTER II

The Opportunity To Be Offended

The Ones We Love Most

On a minute by minute basis, you have the opportunity to be offended. Usually, when an offense comes, it is by the person closest to you.

> *For it was not an enemy that reproached me; then I could have borne it: neither was it he that hated me that did magnify himself against me; then I would have hid myself from him: But it was thou, a man mine equal, my guide, and mine acquaintance.*

*We took sweet counsel together,
and walked unto the house of
God in company.*

Psalm 55:12-14

The offense could be towards the one that
you're married to. It could be that same person
you're with everyday, in the car, at the dinner
table, or on the pew every Sunday at church.
There could even be an offense in your heart
towards that person and you are totally
unaware of it.

I know that's what took place in my own
life. I'm going to be just as transparent with you
as I can be. As most of you know, my husband,
Jerry, is a minister of the Gospel, and he and I
travel and minister all over the world. We both
read the Word every day, spend hours praying,
studying and meditating on God's Word, but
even we are affected by the spirit of offense!

Not too long ago, I began doing this study on the spirit of offense, and I walked into Jerry's office at home and I said something to him about a financial situation we were in, and he said something back to me, and I said, "Well, if you hadn't done this and that, then we would have more than we have right now..." And he looked at me and said, "Well Carolyn, evidently, you've never forgiven me."

I looked at him and said, "Well, Jerry, evidently I haven't."

I continued to say, "Well, I just don't need you. God is my Source of Supply, and He'll provide for me and take care of me."

I had my hands on my hips, my nose in the air, and I huffed out of that room, walked upstairs to my bedroom and thought, "Well, *la ti da* with him. I can take care of myself. I don't need him to meet my needs. I'm married to the Lord. He's my Husband. He'll provide for me."

Have you ever had lousy, rotten attitudes like that? I want you to know, when I got upstairs, and I got quiet before the Lord, the Lord got all over me, and He said, "You know better than this." The Lord showed me where I had been offended. It was an offense I had held in my heart for over three years. Here I was in the ministry, leading intercessory prayer, teaching prayer in Bible School, teaching on the Blood of Jesus, but the whole time, I was allowing this root of bitterness to grow and get deeper and deeper on the inside of me.

Then I found out that offenses can stop you from being fruitful, and I cried, "Oh Lord, I don't want to be barren. I don't want to be stricken with barrenness. I want to bear fruit." I said, "Lord, show me. Teach me. I want You to know I am a teachable person." And that's when He led me into this study on offense.

When I began digging deep into the Word of God and studying everything I could about the spirit of offense, I was amazed to find so much concerning this subject. Evidently, the spirit of offense is something that affects us all and has since the beginning of time.

You could get offended by something someone says to you, or it could even be the way a person looks at you — regardless of the manner in which you become offended, you must resist it like Jesus did.

Offended at the Man of God

There have been many people who have gotten offended at a minister because they didn't agree with the way in which he/she instructed them to do things. In a situation like that, you need to keep your mouth silent, don't voice your complaint to other members in the church, and pray until you feel a peace about your situation and how to handle it. Notice in the story of Naaman, he became offended at the man of God.

Naaman was a mighty man of valour, but he was also a leper. He wrote a letter to the King of Israel asking him for recovery from his leprosy. The King responded saying,

> *Am I God, to kill and to make alive, that this man doth send unto me to recover a man of his leprosy?*
>
> 2 Kings 5:7

Then Elisha, a man of God, said,

> *...Let him come now to me, and he shall know that there is a prophet in Israel. So Naaman came with his horses and with his chariot, and stood at the door of the house of Elisha.*
>
> 2 Kings 5:8

Notice what offended Naaman:

> *And **Elisha sent a messenger** unto him, saying, Go and wash in*

Jordan seven times, and thy flesh shall come again to thee, and thou shalt be clean.

But Naaman was wroth, and went away, and said, Behold I thought, He will surely come out to me, and stand, and call on the name of the Lord his God, and strike his hand over the place, and recover the leper.

*Are not Abana and Pharpar, rivers of Damascus, better than all the waters of Israel? may I not wash in them, and be clean? So he turned and **went away in a rage.***

2 Kings 5:10-12

Naaman became so offended at the prophet because he didn't come out himself and pray over him. He was offended because he sent a messenger to tell him to dip in the Jordan River seven times.

Have you ever gotten offended because you wanted a meeting with the Pastor, but instead he had the Associate Pastor meet with you? It could have been because the Pastor had so many other meetings scheduled and was not able to fit you in that week, but you got offended over it. Naaman got offended because the prophet sent his assistant to meet with him.

Jesus Could Have Been Offended

Jesus is our ultimate example, and He even had the opportunity to be offended. His own mother and brothers called Him a lunatic.

> *When his family heard about this, they went to take charge of him, for they said, **He is out of His mind.***
>
> Mark 3:21
> *New International Version*

Then His brothers and His mother came and, standing outside, they sent word to Him, calling [for] Him.

And a crowd was sitting around him, and they said to Him, Your mother and Your brothers and Your sisters are outside asking for You.

And He replied, Who are My mother and My brothers?

And looking around on those who sat in a circle about Him, He said, See! Here are My mother and My brothers;

For whoever does the things God wills is My brother and sister and mother!

Mark 3:31-35
The Amplified Bible

John 6:60 tells us that many of His own disciples left Him. They didn't agree with what

He was teaching. Jesus was explaining to them that He was the bread from Heaven and whoever eateth of this bread shall live for ever, and notice their reaction.

> *When His disciples heard this, many of them said, This is a hard and difficult and strange saying **(an offensive and unbearable message).** Who can stand to hear it? [Who can be expected to listen to such teaching?]*
>
> John 6:60
> *The Amplified Bible*

> *From that time many of his disciples went back, and walked no more with him.*
>
> John 6:66
> *King James Version*

These were disciples that had followed Jesus. They became offended at His message. Did Jesus have the right to be offended? Yes.

Judas, who had walked with Him for three years, betrayed Him. Peter denied Him, not just once, but three times. Notice what the Word says about Jesus' response to offense:

> *For even to this were you called [it is inseparable from your vocation]. For Christ also suffered for you, leaving you [His personal] example, so that you should follow in His footsteps.*
>
> *He was guilty of no sin; neither was deceit (guile) ever found on His lips.*
>
> *When He was reviled and insulted, He did not revile or offer insult in return; [when] He was abused and suffered, He made no threats [of vengeance]; but He trusted [Himself and everything] to Him Who judges fairly.*
>
> 1 Peter 2:21-23
> *The Amplified Bible*

If anybody had the right to be offended, and to seek revenge, it was Jesus. But He didn't do that. He forgave.

> *Let all bitterness and indignation and wrath (passion, rage, bad temper) and resentment (anger, animosity) and quarreling (brawling, clamor, contention) and slander (evil-speaking, abusive or blasphemous language) be banished from you, with all malice (spite, ill will, or baseness of any kind).*
>
> *And become useful and helpful and kind to one another, tenderhearted (compassionate, understanding, loving-hearted), forgiving one another [readily and freely], as God in Christ forgave you.*
>
> Ephesians 4:31-32
> *The Amplified Bible*

For the most part, we're so quick to want revenge. We're so quick to have contention or to brawl or have passion, rage or a bad temper. None of us have ever experienced what Jesus experienced.

As we see Jesus hanging on the cross, we see people spitting in His face, pulling out His beard, driving nails in His hands and feet, jamming a crown of thorns in His skull. They were beating Him and slapping Him in the face, mocking Him, making fun of Him saying,

Others You saved but Yourself You cannot save. If You truly are the Son of God, come down off the cross and save Yourself.

(Authors paraphrase)

They humiliated Him by stripping Him of all of His clothing, naked for all the world to see. They fed Him vinegar and gall to drink, and He still forgave.

Above all things have intense and unfailing love for one another, for love covers a multitude of sins [forgives and disregards the offenses of others].

1 Peter 4:8
The Amplified Bible

When you think of your situation in comparison to Jesus', it really causes your "offense" to seem petty, doesn't it? Well, it's not petty to God. The hurt or the insult that you experienced is just as real to God as it is to you, and He wants to help you get it out of your heart so you can be what He has called you to be.

CHAPTER III

Voicing The Offense

Touch Not God's Anointed!

In friendships, when people become close, we find out that we all have faults. No one is perfect (except Jesus). The more intimate the relationship, the more the faults become obvious. As I'm sure we have all witnessed many times in church, members notice faults in the church leaders. Or perhaps they become offended at the minister and begin to voice their opinions to others. Soon after, a critical spirit begins to spread, which in many cases, divides a church.

In some instances, a church leader may have

areas in his or her life that need to be changed, but let the Lord be judge over that. Your job is to intercede on his/her behalf. You just keep your heart protected, put a zipper on your mouth and go before the Lord. He'll take care of it. Don't touch God's anointed. The person sitting next to you in church is God's anointed - no matter what you think about them.

You cannot even criticize your own mate because when you do, you are touching God's anointed. If you sow strife, you will reap strife. Usually, we are unaware that the offense has entered into our heart and then the root of bitterness is barely noticed as it develops.

> *...lest any root of bitterness springing up trouble you, and thereby many be defiled.*
>
> Hebrews 12:15

In other words, we are to have a constant watch, and guard over our mouths. We must examine our heart and open ourselves to the Lord for only His Word can determine the thought and intentions of our heart.

Spreading the Spirit of Offense

In Ezekiel 28, we have a picture of how Lucifer became offended at God because he wanted to get all the praise. He felt like God had been given enough praise and that he had served God long enough - it was time to receive praise himself. He wanted worship and recognition for who he was and what he had done. Have you ever had those thoughts?

Lucifer became dissatisfied and offended at God. What did he do? Because of pride and because he felt he should be adored, he began to spread his offense. I'm sure he went to the entire angelic hosts and began to voice his displeasure. He expressed that he should be like God and be exalted above the Most High God.

He began to voice his complaint to the point that he convinced one-third of the angelic hosts that he should be praised, worshipped and exalted. There was war in heaven and a third of the angels were cast out of heaven and fell with Lucifer (Ezekiel 28:14-19).

This is a classic example of how one offended person can spread his/her offense to other people in the church, fellow employees, family members, or neighbors and cause division. Many times, people begin to complain against the leader and feel like the leader is not doing what he should do, and it causes the offense to be spread to everyone around.

I want you to be aware of the traps that Satan is using to catch you. Since you are already knowledgeable of his devices, then get a step ahead of him. Don't allow the spirit of offense to trap you. Don't spread that spirit to others. Release it and move on.

Learn to Guard Your Mouth

We have to be so careful with our mouths. We've got to learn to put a guard over our mouths and keep our opinions to ourselves. Trafficking an offense or voicing what you think ought to be changed is the very spirit that caused Satan to be cast out of heaven. We have to put a guard and a watch over our mouth so that we are not taking that offense from one person to another.

When we are offended, we generally want to take that offense to someone else. Why? So we can get sympathy. "Do you know what they did to me? Do you know what they said about me? Do you know how they hurt me? Do you know how they offended me?" We tend to go to other people for sympathy rather than going to the person who offended us and settling it once and for all. My husband says that when you talk about your problem, it only magnifies it.

Cain went to his brother, instead of seeking God, and began to voice his offense. He began to voice his hurt, and talk about how he felt treated unfairly.

Don't you know I labored with my hands? Don't you know the hours, days and months that I was out there working in the fields? I labored with my hands to cause this fruit to come so that I could present it to God, and then God rejected my offering!

(Author's paraphrase)

This was God's response through his brother to Cain:

If you do well, will you not be accepted? And if you do not do well, sin crouches at your door; its desire is for you, and you must master it.

Genesis 4:7

The Amplified Bible

Abel was trying to tell Cain that if he had done what God required, God would have accepted his offering. *...And if you do not well, sin crouches at your door.* In other words, Satan is waiting to have you. *...It's desire is for you but you must master it.* The picture here is this: when we get offended and don't immediately get rid of that offense, as soon as we walk out the door, Satan has captured us.

It's like a lion waiting to pounce on you as you walk out the door, if you continue to harbor an offense in your heart. Sin (or Satan) is waiting at the door to see if you did or didn't forgive. If you didn't, the second you come out of the door, he has captured you. You have fallen into his pit.

Genesis says, "Cain talked to his brother." But it doesn't say what his brother said. I'm going to suppose that Abel didn't sympathize with Cain one bit. And perhaps Abel told his brother just exactly how it was. When people are offended, they often don't want to hear the truth. Consequently, Cain became offended at his own brother because he didn't like the answer. He didn't like the response.

That's how human nature is. If you went to someone saying, "Do you know what she said about me? She really insulted me..." And that person responded to you saying, "You need to forgive them. They didn't mean it like that when they said it." I want you to know, nine times out of ten, we would get offended at them too. That's not what we want to hear! Now, we're offended at two people. It's multiplying. It doesn't just affect one person, one offense can affect a multitude of people.

When Abel told Cain, "Just do what God required and it will be all right." He became so offended at his brother that he premeditated murder. He took him out in the field and killed him. Obviously, Abel didn't agree with him and say, "Well, you poor darling. It's God's fault. It's

God who should be ashamed for treating you this way." No, he rebuked him and told him the truth.

The next time someone says something to you that insults you or hurts your feelings, purposely strive to resist that spirit of offense from coming into your heart. Don't say a word to anyone else about your "opportunity" to be offended, and immediately pray for that person. Just see how differently you'll feel. Think about how proud your Heavenly Father is when you resist the opportunity to be offended and how upset and disappointed the Devil is that you didn't fall for his trap!

Envy and Jealousy

Offense can lead to envy and jealousy as in the story of Cain and Abel. I want you to notice the relationship of David and Saul and how the spirit of offense entered Saul.

Then Samuel took the horn of oil and anointed David in the midst of his brothers; and the Spirit of the Lord came mightily upon David from that day forward. And Samuel arose and went to Ramah.

I Samuel 16:13
The Amplified Bible

You know the story how Goliath was provoking the army of God and David saw that there were rewards to be gained if one could kill Goliath. Amazingly, he slew Goliath and became son of the king. He married the king's daughter, came into covenant with the king's son, and he began living in the king's palace. He gained a great deal that day.

And one day, as Saul and David were returning from battle, there were songs being sung by the women as they entered into the city. They were singing, "Saul has slain his thousands but David has slain his tens of thousands." And at that moment, a spirit of offense entered into Saul's heart. He became jealous and envious of David.

> *... And Saul [jealously] eyed David from that day forward ... And he raved [madly] in his house ...*
>
> 1 Samuel 18:9,10
> *The Amplified Bible*

This infuriated Saul and caused him to despise David so much that on two occasions he tried to kill him in the palace. The spirit of offense caused him to want to kill his own son-in-law.

With 3,000 warriors, he chased David all over the country. Eventually, David entered into the city of Nob, and the priest fed him and clothed his men. When Saul heard about it, he had all the priests and all of their families slaughtered and killed.

An offense is like a seed that grows and grows. It must be purposely dealt with and uprooted. Notice what took place from the spirit of offense.

David cried unto Saul saying,

> *See my father, see the skirt of your robe in my hand! Since I cut off the skirt of your robe and did not kill you, you know and see that there is no evil or treason in my hands. I have not sinned against you, yet you hunt my life to take it.*

> 1 Samuel 24:11
> *The Amplified Bible*

He was saying, "See what I have done for you. All I've ever done is love you, serve you, devote my life to you. There is no evil or treason in my hands. Why are you seeking my life to kill me?"

Saul went away. But, he began meditating on it, thinking about it, dwelling on it. Then the spirit took over his life once again, and he began chasing David throughout the land.

In order to be accepted by Saul, David tried to prove his loyalty to him. But only a short time later, we see Saul chasing him again throughout the land in order to kill him. Then one night, David and one of his soldiers quietly crept into Saul's camp.

> *Then said Abishai to David, God has given your enemy into your hands this day. Now therefore let me smite him to the earth at once with one stroke of the spear, and I will not strike him twice.*
>
> I Samuel 26:8
> *The Amplified Bible*

David's soldier is begging him, "Let me take his life. I'm only going to have to strike once and my spear will go all the way through him."

I want you to listen to David's response.

*David said to Abishai, Do not destroy him; for **who can raise his hand against the Lord's anointed, and be guiltless?***

David said, As the Lord lives, [He] will smite him; or his day will come to die or he will go down in battle and perish.

The Lord forbid that I should raise my hand against the Lord's anointed; but take now the spear that is at his head, and the bottle of water, and let us go.

1 Samuel 26:9-11
The Amplified Bible

David would not kill Saul even though Saul was trying to kill David at every turn in the road. Saul was chasing David constantly trying to kill him, but again David's response was, "I will not raise my hand against the Lord's anointed." David was a godly man who respected the anointing on Saul's life. He would not touch God's anointed.

In fact, later when David heard about Saul and Jonathan being killed, he didn't throw a party and celebrate at their destruction. Do you know what he did? He mourned. He wept. He called for all of Israel to mourn. He even instructed that the man who killed Saul be put to death.

> *Tell it not in Gath, announce it not in the streets of Ashkelon, lest the daughters of the Philistines rejoice, lest the daughters of the uncircumcised exult.*
>
> 2 Samuel 1:20
> *The Amplified Bible*

David wrote a song in honor of Saul and Jonathan. He encourged the people to not voice this tragedy because the enemy would rejoice over it. From this example, we see a person, David, who could have been greatly offended, but chose not to. Instead he was deeply sorrowful.

In other words, even if you have the "right" to be offended because you are not the one who is in the wrong - don't yield to that spirit. The spirit of offense affects you, not the one who hurt you.

CHAPTER **IV**

Building Walls

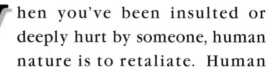

hen you've been insulted or deeply hurt by someone, human nature is to retaliate. Human nature says, "You hurt my feelings; therefore, I resent you. You're going to pay for this. I'm not going to speak to you. I'm going to build up that wall of protection around me and you're never going to get that close to me again." And the walls go up.

Jesus said, *Love your enemies, bless them that curse you, do good to them that hate you, and pray for them which despitefully use you and persecute you...* (Matthew 5:44). Do you know how hard it is to pray for those who have spoken ugly about you? When people have offended you, hurt you, and wounded you and you're supposed to sincerely pray for them - that's a step of faith! We have to do what David did in Psalms 35:11,12 *(Amplified)*:

> *Malicious and unrighteous witnesses rise up; they ask me of things that I know not.*
>
> *They reward me evil for good to my personal bereavement.*

These men were trying to destroy David, but notice what he did in return:

Verse 13:

> *But as for me, when they were sick my clothing was sackcloth; I afflicted myself with fasting, and I prayed with head bowed on my breast.*
>
>   *The Amplified Bible*

Praying for someone who has hurt you seems like a joke. Why would you want to do that? Usually, we don't even want to think about that person, much less pray for them. But this is what David said:

> *I behaved as if grieving for my friend or my brother; I bowed down in sorrow, as one who bewails his mother.*

> Psalm 35:14
> *The Amplified Bible*

If your mother, father, brother or sister is sick or in need, what do you do? You try to be the first one there to help them, pray for them, and get them out of the situation that they are in, right? You will even give your very life to help them. I only have one sister, and anytime she's ever had a need and called me for help, I want you to know I get there as quick as I can to offer help and support.

Well, according to the Word of God, this is what we should do for our enemies as well. We should go to the aid of those who speak evil against us. Sound crazy? You'd be surprised how much peace and calmness fills your heart and mind when you do this. Just releasing offenses from your heart will completely revive your spirit.

There are many people today who have been offended at church and never seem to get back into relationships with people or ever faithfully attend church again. How many church members have you seen leave offended? They leave the church and go from one church to another one, but they are never satisfied. They continue to live their lives with an offended heart, and they never fully bear the fruit that God wants them to bear.

> *Behold, thou hast driven me out*
> *this day from the face of the earth;*
> *and from thy face shall I be hid;*

*and I shall be a fugitive and a
vagabond in the earth; and it
shall come to pass, that every one
that findeth me shall slay me.*

Genesis 4:14

I want you to notice the progression of the
spirit of offense. A person begins to have a chip
on their shoulder. They begin to build walls of
defense up around themselves because they've
been hurt. Eventually, the walls become thicker
and thicker. "I'm not going to be hurt like that
again," they say. The walls that they are building are to protect them from being vulnerable
again.

There are many church members who are
offended because the pastor has never asked
them to preach or to sing or play their instru-
ment in the church. They walk around harboring an offense in their heart. "Well, I've been
coming to this church for years, and they've

never asked me to sing. Not one time! And they know the gift and talent that I have." So, they get offended.

We have to constantly guard our thoughts against anything like that. It always starts as a thought that enters your mind, and you have the ability to refuse that thought or dwell on it until it becomes an offense.

> *A brother offended is harder to be won than a strong city: and their contentions are like the bars of a castle.*
>
> Proverbs 18:19

The Amplified Bible:

> *A brother offended is harder to be won over than a strong city, and [their] contentions separate them like the bars of a castle.*

Notice it doesn't say that they can't be won, but that they are harder to win than a strong city. When we figure in the anointing factor, those walls of offense can come down. Remember the story of the walls of Jericho — they came down!

The walls of Jericho were so thick just like the walls people have built around themselves. That was an impenetrateable city. People could not get into the city because of the thickness of those walls. It wasn't until the anointing of God came on the scene as they were marching around those walls, that they came down! It's the same thing with the walls that you may have built up in your life. God's anointing can bring them down and set you free.

I know there have been instances in my own life where people have offended me or I have offended them. I didn't know that I had offended them, but I found that there was a distance in our relationship. Eventually, I began to wonder, "What have I done to them?" Not knowing what I had done to offend them, I just prayed in the spirit. When that happens you can confront that person and simply ask, "Have I done something to hurt or offend you? If so, I want to ask for your forgiveness."

When you realize the seriousness of having a spirit of offense in your heart, you'll want to quickly get it out. We are required by the Word of God to forebear, to cover that offense and forgive.

The anointing can be coupled together with revelation knowledge to destroy those walls of offense and bring down those barriers. Even if the person you offended is not quick to forgive you, keep praying in the spirit. Don't give up. I want you to know those walls can come down and relationships can be restored.

> *And this I pray, that your love*
> *may abound yet more and more*

in knowledge and in all judgment;

That ye may approve things that are excellent; that ye may be sincere and without offence till the day of Christ;

Being filled with the fruits of righteousness, which are by Jesus Christ, unto the glory and praise of God.

Philippians 1:9-11

God is here to deliver us and to set us free. You may have been deeply wounded and hurt, and I would never make light of your situation. There may have been things happen in your life that have caused deep scars on the inside of you. You may have had a father abandon you, or been physically or mentally abused by someone, and you've never been able to forgive that person. Well, today is the day for your deliverance. You can't do anything to make them apologize or "pay" for what they did to you. But you can forgive them and move on in your life. Don't let their mistake stop you from being successful. It's time to forgive them.

Harboring Unforgiveness

Harboring unforgiveness in our lives can not only stop our progress in the things of God, but it can delay God's perfect plan for our lives. You can literally wind up wasting years of your life simply because of an offense toward someone that you never released. We see this taking place in the life of Absalom.

In 2 Samuel 13, David's son, Amnon, committed a wicked and evil crime against his half sister Tamar (Absalom's sister). He pretended to be sick and asked his father to send Tamar in to feed him and take care of him. He sent the servants away, and he defiled her. He molested her. He had destroyed her life forever. She would never be able to hold her head up in public without feeling shame.

Because of Absalom's compassion for his sister, he took her in to his home to take care of her. I can just imagine Tamar, if she was like any average woman, crying miserably day in and day out over this devastation in her life. Her life was deplorable, wretched, and worthless. A life lived in despair. She had been severely violated. The more she wept over the situation, the more it ate Absalom up on the inside. This was somewhat understandable, right? Well, notice what the effect of an offense had on Absalom's life.

This hatred for Amnon grew so strong in Absalom that he thought certainly his father, King David, would feel the same. However, although David was infuriated, he did absolutely nothing about it. This enraged Absalom to the point that bitterness began to overtake his life. Revenge was all he thought about day and night.

You know the story. He asked his father if he could have all his brothers come to a party at his home and he threw a party for all the King's sons and plotted where he would have his brother, Amnon, killed the night of the party. The Bible says that he had Amnon killed. His revenge was carried out, but then he had to flee for his life. He fled to Gesher where he stayed for three years.

Notice Absalom walks around for two years with this bitterness, this hatred, this offense in his heart planning to murder Amnon. Then for three years he was in exile running. That's five years of his life literally consumed with a spirit of offense.

Joab tried to persuade King David to let Absalom come back home, but David still denied Joab's request to meet with Absalom in person. The Word says that two more years went by before David finally agreed to let Absalom come home and be restored as his son again. So, seven years went by. Seven years lived in torment. Absalom's life was eaten up and consumed with revenge. His life was consumed with bitterness and hatred. Seven years were wasted with nothing to be proud of - no accomplishments.

Putting on a Facade

The offense in Absalom's heart grew stronger and deeper. 2 Samuel 13:22 says,

> *...Absalom spake unto his brother Amnon neither good nor bad: for Absalom hated Amnon...*

In other words, Amnon couldn't tell what he was thinking. He put on a facade. He had the appearance of someone that you would like. Absalom was good at cover-ups. Many people, like Absalom, can put on a facade and disguise their offense. An offended spirit is like a magnet. People are drawn to it. In the example with

Absalom, people began to gravitate to him to voice their hurts and offenses. It's a very interesting example from the Word of God from which you should continue to read and learn.

He sat at the city gates listening to each criticism, accusation, objection and charge against the king. He would talk to them. He would give them his time. He would say, "If I was king, I would do it this way. If I was leader, I wouldn't do it that way. It would be better if I were king. I would have time for you. We would change this. We would have this program." (Author's paraphrase)

He would listen to suggestions making it appear that he cared more for them than the king did.

> *Thus Absalom did to all Israel who came to the king for judgement. So Absalom stole the hearts of the men of Israel.*
>
> 2 Samuel 15:6
> *The Amplified Bible*

Have you ever heard the pharse, "Pity loves a party"? We see a classic example of that in this story. People enjoy sharing their misery with anyone who will listen. Absalom tried to overthrow his father's kingdom with an army made up of discontented, bitter, unhappy men. The Word says that King David had to flee Jerusalem for his life. While pursuing David, Absalom was killed.

Even with his own son chasing to kill him, David still had a heart like God and ordered that no one harm his son. He would not allow a spirit of offense to come in his heart even though he had ample opportunity to do so. On the other hand, Absalom, as a young man, was killed because of the offense that he allowed to grow and consume his life. He refused to release it, and ended up corrupt.

Many of us have been hurt, offended and even violated like the story mentioned, but you cannot allow a spirit of offense to ruin your life and your destiny. I realize it is something that you must diligently work on getting out of your heart, but it is a life or death decision. Do you want to be held back all of your life? Or do you want to be the success that God has designed for you to be? You, and only you, make the decision.

C H A P T E R

V

The Consequence Of An Offense

Jesus was very explicit in seeing to it that we understand the danger of harboring unforgiveness. After reading this parable, there should be no question of the consequences of having an offense in your heart.

> *Therefore is the kingdom of heaven likened unto a certain king, which would take account of his servants. And when he had begun to reckon, one was brought unto him, which owed him ten thousand talents.*

But forasmuch as he had not to pay, his lord commanded him to be sold, and his wife, and children, and all that he had, and payment to be made. The servant therefore fell down, and worshipped him, saying, Lord, have patience with me, and I will pay thee all.

Then the lord of that sevant was moved with compassion, and loosed him, and forgave him the debt. But the same servant went out, and found one of his fellowservants, which owed him an hundred pence: and he laid hands on him, and took him by the throat, saying, Pay me that thou owest.

And his fellowservant fell down at his feet, and besought him, saying, Have patience with me, and I will pay thee all. And he would not: but went and cast him into prison, till he should pay the debt.

So when his fellowservants saw what was done, they were very sorry, and came and told unto their lord all that was done. Then his lord, after that he had called him, said unto him, O thou wicked servant, I forgave thee all that debt, because thou desiredst me:

Shouldest not thou also have had compassion on thy fellowservant, even as I had pity on thee? And his lord was wroth, and delivered him to the tormentors, till he should pay all that was due unto him.

So likewise shall my heavenly Father do also unto you, if ye

*from your hearts forgive not every
one his brother their trespasses.*

Matthew 18:23-35

No matter how great the hurt or the
offense, if we don't freely forgive from the
heart, we will be turned over to the tormentors.
This is just as clear as the nose on our face.

We can go to church, pay our tithes, go to
prayer meetings, and we can preach and declare
the Word of God, but if we continue to hold
and harbor offense in our hearts, the Word says,

*So also My heavenly Father will
deal with every one of you if you
do not freely forgive your brother
from your heart his offenses.*

Matthew 18:35
The Amplified Bible

Do you understand how deadly it is to hold offenses in your heart? You're doing no one any good, only hurting yourself and possibly your eternity. If you do not freely forgive from the heart, then Jesus cannot forgive you. It's the Word. This is scripture. I didn't write it.

I'm endeavoring, to the best of my ability, to get this over to you as seriously as the Lord got it over to me. He said to me, "Carolyn, you cannot be forgiven if you cannot forgive. You're going to have to pay the original unpayable debt."

Haven't you carried certain things around with you long enough? The Lord wants you free of it all. He wants you totally and completely free!

> *For verily I say unto you that whosoever shall say unto this mountain, Be thou removed, and be thou cast into the sea; and shall*

not doubt in his heart, but shall believe that those things which he saith shall come to pass; he shall have whatsoever he saith.

Therefore I say unto you, What things soever ye desire, when ye pray, believe that ye receive them, and ye shall have them.

*And when ye stand praying, **forgive,** if ye have **aught** against any: that your Father also which is in heaven may forgive you your trespasses.*

But if ye do not forgive, neither will your Father which is in heaven forgive your trespasses.

Mark 11:23-26

It's clear Jesus meant what He said.

For if ye forgive men their trespasses, your heavenly Father will also forgive you: But if ye forgive not men their trespasses, neither will your Father forgive your trespasses.

Matthew 6:14,15

...Forgive and ye shall be forgiven.

Luke 6:37

Forgiveness is a debt we owe, but when you forgive, it cancels that debt. For us to receive from God, we must forgive.

An Unfruitful Life

So David and all the house of Israel brought up the ark of the Lord with shouting, and with the sound of the trumpet. As the ark of the Lord came into the city of

David, Michal Saul's daughter looked out of the window, and saw king David leaping and dancing before the Lord; and she despised him in her heart.

2 Samuel 6:15,16

Notice how David's wife, Michal, reacted when she saw David dancing before the Lord. She didn't run up to him and give him a big hug around the neck and a kiss on the cheek, she despised him in her heart.

Then David returned to bless his household. And [his wife] Michal daughter of Saul came out to meet David and said, How glorious was the king of Israel today, who stripped himself of his kingly robes and uncovered himself in the eyes of his servants' maids as one of the worthless fellows shamelessly uncovers himself!

2 Samuel 6:20

She was so ashamed of him, she was offended at what he did — he had embarrassed her. Look at verse 21. *The Amplified Bible:*

David said to Michal, It was before the Lord, Who chose me above your father and all his house to appoint me as prince over Israel, the people of the Lord. Therefore will I make merry [in pure enjoyment] before the Lord.

You have to read between the lines here. I can just imagine by her response, how offended and disgusted she was with him. He had embarrassed her. A wife has a way of saying things to her husband. She knows which buttons to push. We can say things with just a little edge to our voice - that can set off World War III. Am I right?

Well, I believe that's what Michal did that day with David. She went up to him and said, "How dare you, you're the king! You've stripped yourself as some worthless fellow out in the streets. You have humiliated me! You have embarrassed me!" (Author's paraphrase)

She gave him a piece of her mind. And notice his response: *It was before the Lord who chose me above your father...* I mean, he's telling her off. He said, "God chose me before your own father..." He's putting her down. There were some words exchanged that day, probably quite a few more than what we see written here.

> *I will be still more lightly esteemed than this, and will humble and lower myself in my own sight [and yours]. But by the*

> *maids you mentioned, I will be*
> *held in honor. And Michal the*
> *daughter of Saul had no child to*
> *the day of her death.*
>
> 2 Samuel 6:22, 23
> *The Amplified Bible*

A seminary student pointed out to me one time that the reason she didn't have children was because David was never intimate with her again after that day.

Whether that's true or not, you can decide. Because of an offense in her heart, their marriage never reached the full potential that God had intended for it to reach. Think about that. It could be the case in your marriage. Go back and look at these verses here. Quite possibly David became offended at her, and she became offended at him and there was no more intimacy between the two of them which prevented them from ever having children.

What does this speak of allegorically? You get offended in Jesus and what Jesus is doing to others, and you will be smitten with barrenness because the Bridegroom won't have intimacy with you. You will be barren in your spirit, barren in your life, barren in your ministry, and barren in your church.

Keep Your Opinions Silent

We may not totally agree with the way certain people minister - their style of delivery, what they were born with, their mannerisms, etc., but it is not our place to judge, to criticize, or to voice our opinion to anyone else.

There are ministers on TV that I can't watch. I am unable to glean from or receive from their style of delivery like I can from others. I have to continually pray as I watch them because I just don't care for yelling and screaming. I don't care for spit flying and sweat streaming. I love to see a preacher get anointed and run back and forth in the anointing. I'm not talking about that. I love to see anointed, powerful sermons, but there are just certain types of ministry that don't minister to me like others. But that's why there are all types. God uses different styles of ministry to reach different styles of people.

I'm just being honest with you because I want you to understand that you are not the only one who has these thoughts. If I'm flipping through the TV channels, and I see a particular minister that I may not agree with the way he/she does things, I want you to know that I put a guard over my mouth. It's better to turn the television off than to allow myself to become critical.

I don't allow those thoughts and feelings to get down inside of me. I'm not going to allow myself to be offended and critical. I don't want to be stricken with barrenness. I want to continually have intimacy with the Father God so I can bear fruit that remains. We must keep our heart protected. We must not be offended. We must keep the spirit of offense out.

We have to choose not to be offended. It's a choice we make minute by minute. You can finish reading this book and instantly have the opportunity to be offended. It's a choice we make daily.

In the story with David and Michal, I'm sure most of us can relate to being insulted by our spouse. Are there things that your spouse did that you just can't seem to forget? It may have even been ten years ago, and you're still walking around with that in your heart. Well, you are the one being hurt when you hold an offense.

Your life will stop progressing because of the offense, not your spouse's life. You have got to make a decision once and for all that today is the day that you will release all unforgiveness and the offenses in your heart. And you must make a quality decision to **never, never, never** bring up that offense again. Don't talk about it. Don't think about it. Don't mention it. Forget it. It's over with. It's been uprooted and removed out of your heart. You are free from offenses in Jesus' Name.

CHAPTER

VI

The Effect On Your Harvest

Are you sowing financial seed but failing to reap the harvest that God says you are entitled to? You can sow seed, and give your tithe consistently; however, according to the Word, it doesn't matter how much you give, if there is offense in your heart, your sowing won't bear fruit.

This could be the very answer you've been looking for as to why you are sowing much but reaping little. It's time to get the offense out. Offenses not only affect your growth in the Lord, your success in life, and your destiny, but they also have a direct effect on your finances.

And now art thou cursed from the earth, which hath opened her mouth to receive thy brother's blood from thy hand;

When thou tillest the ground, it shall not henceforth yield unto thee her strength; a fugitive and a vagabond shalt thou be in the earth.

Genesis 4:11,12

We saw in the story of Cain and Abel that because of an offense, Cain's life began to dry up. He was offended, and his life was no longer fruitful. He was a wanderer, a vagabond, continually going here and there and never bearing fruit in his life.

Do you believe we are in the time of supernatural increase and restoration? I believe we are, and God wants us to reap the full potential from our giving.

And those sown on good (well-adapted) soil are the ones who hear the Word and receive and accept and welcome it and bear fruit - some thirty times as much as was sown, some sixty times as much and some [even] a hundred times as much.

Mark 4:20
The Amplified Bible

Now the Word of God says that if you sow seed you're going to receive a thirty, sixty or a hundred fold return. Carolyn didn't write it. So why aren't we receiving that kind of harvest on **every** seed that we sow? It could be because of an insult or an offense that we've held in our hearts towards someone who hurt us.

*And when ye stand praying, forgive, **if ye have aught against***

> ***any:*** *that your Father also which*
> *is in heaven may forgive you*
> *your trespasses. But if ye do not*
> *forgive, neither will your Father*
> *which is in heaven forgive your*
> *trespasses.*
>
>   Mark 11:25

God is plainly revealing to us that unforgiveness can hinder our prayers from being answered. Your behavior can stop your harvest from manifesting. *Aught* in this context can be defined as "a grudge, resentment, bitterness or malice." If you are holding a grudge against someone, then the Father can't forgive you.

Malice is defined as "deep-seated animosity, hostile feelings, ill-will wished upon another or bitterness." Can you identify with these feelings? If so, then that would explain why your harvest has been stopped. You cannot expect God to multiply your seed and increase you financially if you are holding a grudge against someone. It doesn't matter how bad they hurt you, you will not go forward in life until the offense is removed.

Bitterness in your heart is like a root that goes down deep. It can't just be pulled up one time. You have to keep an eye on it. You have to dig down deep into your spirit and vigorously work at getting that root of bitterness out. It's the same thing in a garden. You have to work hard at pulling roots up, especially weeds. Well, bitterness is like a weed, and if you don't keep manicuring your garden (heart), then those weeds will come up automatically without you even noticing it. Weeds just appear overnight. They grow so fast and eventually can crowd out the other plants.

Don't let the root of bitterness crowd out the good fruit in your life. You have the fruit of the spirit abiding on the inside of you which is love, joy, peace, longsuffering, gentleness, goodness, faith, meekness, and temperence.

You will have the opportunity to be offended every day, but you have to make a quality decision to not let anyone offend you. Start digging up those weeds. You may have weeds that need to be pulled out from an insult that occurred twenty years ago. Well, start digging.

> *You have sown much, but you have reaped little; you eat, but you do not have enough; you drink, but you do not have your fill; you clothe yourselves, but no one is warm; and he who earns wages has earned them to put them in a bag with holes in it.*

> *Thus says the Lord of Hosts: Consider your ways (your previous and present conduct) and how you have fared.*

Haggai 1:6,7
The Amplified Bible

According to Haggai, if you are sowing much and reaping little, then you need to consider your ways. Not God's ways. Obviously, there is something about your life that needs to be changed. It could be that you are offended. *Ways* is defined as "course of action, methods and manners, conduct and behavior." In other words, if you are sowing much, but reaping little, then it's time to consider your behavior. Your behavior has a profound effect on the kind of harvest you receive.

> *You have heard that it was said to the men of old, You shall not kill, and whoever kills shall be liable to and unable to escape the punishment imposed by the court.*
>
> *But I say to you that everyone who continues to be angry with his brother or harbors malice (enmity of heart) against him shall be liable to and unable to*

escape the punishment imposed by the court; and whoever speaks contemptuously and insultingly to his brother shall be liable to and unable to escape the punishment imposed by the Sanhedrin, and whoever says, You cursed fool! [You empty-headed idiot!] shall be liable to and unable to escape the hell (Gehenna) of fire.

So if when you are offering your gift at the altar you there remember that your brother has any [grievance] against you, Leave your gift at the altar and go. First make peace with your brother, and then come back and present your gift. Come to terms quickly with your accuser...

Matthew 5:21-25
The Amplified Bible

We have found the answer to why we sow much and reap little. It's us. We've got to release all bitterness from our hearts. Do you believe we are in the end time? Do you believe that time is speeding up and we don't have much time left here on planet earth? I believe that we only have a few years left. If that is in fact true, then God is going to speed up the sowing and reaping process so we can finance the Gospel to the world. We've got to have the finances to publish the Gospel to all nations so we can bring Jesus back. So, let's not allow offenses in our heart to stop the sowing and reaping process in our lives. We've got work to do. We've got to share Jesus with others.

Determine to forgive those who have trespassed against you no matter how minor or how severe the attack was. Don't allow their insult to effect your harvest. Release all offenses in your life that are keeping you in bondage and are hindering the return on your giving that the Lord wants you to receive.

CHAPTER VII

Confronting The Offense

Blessed are the peacemakers for they shall be called the children of God.

Matthew 5:9

A peacemaker will go in love and confront, bringing truth, so that healing and restoration can come. A peacemaker does not put on a facade and call you a friend, then talk against you behind your back. How many times have we been around someone that has offended us, and we put on a fake smile and act like everything is OK, when on the inside we are seething?

When I began studying the spirit of offense, I had to go to my husband and ask him to forgive me because of the offense in my heart that I had harbored for several years. A peacemaker desires sincerity, truth and love.

I have never been a confronter. Sometimes it's easier to just cover up things. Sometimes you want to put on a false face and a fake smile, and therefore your relationship is not deep and rich like it should be. But I decided, I refuse to hide offenses. I refuse to allow a root of bitterness to spring up on the inside of me.

> ***Strive to live in peace*** *with everybody and pursue that consecration and holiness without which no one will [ever] see the Lord.*
>
> *Exercise foresight and be on the watch to look [after one another], to see that no one falls back from*

*and fails to secure God's grace (His unmerited favor and spiritual blessing), in order that no **root of resentment (rancor, bitterness or hatred) shoots forth and causes trouble and bitter torment, and the many become contaminated and defiled by it** -*

Hebrews 12:14,15
The Amplified Bible

The Living Bible says,

*Try to stay out of all quarrels and seek to live a clean and holy life, for one who is not holy will not see the Lord. Look after each other so that not one of you will fail to find God's best blessings. **Watch out that no bitterness takes root among you, for as it springs up it causes deep trouble, hurting many in their spiritual lives.***

In the story with my husband, for over three years I was walking around thinking I was anointed, and thinking I was in the will of God, but I was defiled the whole time. Bitterness is a root. And if the roots are nourished, watered, fed and protected, then they increase in strength and they increase in depth. If roots are not dealt with quickly, they are hard to pull up. The strength of the offense will continue to grow. The Bible says the person who does not pursue peace by releasing offense will eventually be defiled. *Defiled* means soiled, filthy, polluted.

Retaliate or Forgive?

In Luke 9 we see an opportunity for Jesus to become offended, but let's see how He reacted. Jesus was preparing for a meeting in Samaria, and He sent His crusade team ahead to prepare the way and get everything ready to announce the meeting. As Jesus approaches the city, His team meets Him outside of town and says, "The Samaritans have refused to let You come in."

(Author's paraphrase)   Because of the Samaritan's attitude, Jesus' disciples wanted to call fire down from heaven on them. They wanted to burn them up. They had scriptures and proof that it had been done before (in the story of Elijah; 1 Kings 18:19-40), so they thought they had the right to do it, too.

They wanted to burn them to a crisp. But notice Jesus' response to their disappointing news:

> *But he turned and rebuked them, and said, Ye know not what manner of spirit ye are of.*
>
> *For the Son of man is not come to destroy men's lives, but to save them. And they went to another village.*
>
> Luke 9:55,56

I want you to notice that it didn't even phase Jesus. It didn't alter where He was going or the course He was called to do. It didn't even slow Him down one bit. He didn't retaliate. He didn't want to strike back. He simply said, "You do not know what spirit you are of." And He turned and rebuked them. That was His response. Now, when we've been offended or we've been hurt, we can choose to either retaliate with vengeance or we can choose to cover over and forebear. Which are you going to do?

When your spouse says something that could hurt you, you can either strike back with an ugly remark, or do what Jesus did — move on! Confront the offense and deal with it immediately. Don't let roots grow up on the inside of you for years and years and never deal with it. Don't stop your destiny simply because you were hurt by someone years ago.

I made the decision that I would no longer wonder if I've offended someone. Now I go right up to that person and politely ask them. I want all offenses dealt with immediately in my life so I can progress in my walk with God. I don't want anything holding me back.

After reading this book and studying the spirit of offense, hopefully you'll become more aware of opportunities to become offended and you'll learn to resist them. On the other hand, hopefully you'll become more aware of opportunities that come for you to offend someone and repel them as well. Confront the offense and move forward.

VIII

CHAPTER

The Choice Is Yours

VIII

You have a choice. You can choose to be offended, to carry that offense with you everywhere you go for years and years. You can choose to voice that offense to everyone in order to obtain sympathy. You can be what the Devil wants you to be — offended. Or you can **choose not** to be offended.

> *For even hereunto were ye called: because Christ also suffered for us, leaving us an example, that ye should follow his steps;*
>
> *Who did no sin, neither was guile found in his mouth:*

*Who, when he was reviled, reviled
not again; when he suffered, he
threatened not; but committed
himself to him that judgeth right-
eously:*

1 Peter 2:21-23

That's what God has called us to do. You'll
notice in the life of Noah, where two of his sons
were concerned, that Noah had committed a sin
but these two sons decided to cover their
father's sin. What did they do? They didn't
look on the sin. They walked backwards to
where their father was and wouldn't look on
the sin. They didn't announce it to "prime
time." They didn't send it to all the Christian
tabloids to get it put in the magazines. They
didn't tell it from neighbor to neighbor and
from minister to minister to get it spread like
wildfire throughout the Body of Christ, instead
they covered him up.

Many times we feel like the injustice done to us was too harsh for us to forgive. Especially in the case of someone being violated in some form, but according to Matthew 18:21-22 we must forgive our trespassers because God, in His mercy, has forgiven us. Notice the illustration:

Moreover if thy brother shall trespass against thee, go and tell him his fault between thee and him alone: if he shall hear thee, thou hast gained thy brother. But if he will not hear thee, then take with thee one or two more, that in the mouth of two or three witnesses every word may be established.

And if he shall neglect to hear them, tell it unto the church: but if he neglect to hear the church, let him be unto thee as an heathen man and a publican.

Verily I say unto you, Whatsoever ye shall bind on earth shall be bound in heaven: and whatsoever ye shall loose on earth shall be loosed in heaven.

Again I say unto you, That if two of you shall agree on earth as touching any thing that they shall ask, it shall be done for them of my Father which is in heaven. For where two or three are gathered together in my name, there am I in the midst of them.

Then came Peter to him, and said, Lord, how oft shall my brother sin against me, and I forgive him? till seven times? Jesus saith unto him, I say not unto thee, Until seven times: but, Until seventy times seven.

Matthew 18:15-22

An Act of Your Will

It is an act of your will to forgive those who have hurt you. The Word of God is the standard by which we are entitled to live, and it plainly says that you must forgive and release offenses from your heart. For me, once it is pointed out in the Word of God, I get determined real quick to change.

I choose to be a person who is not offended. That's the key. We have the choice to let things hurt us, or to forgive and move on. When you choose not to be offended and begin to pray for that person, just as you would for a very close friend or a relative, the anointing of God will come and deliver and destroy those yokes, and a relationship can be built.

Romans 14:13 describes what our attitude should be:

> *Let us not therefore judge one another any more: but judge this rather, that no man put a stumblingblock or an occasion to fall in his brother's way.*

Our maturity level will determine how well we handle offense. On a different note, we need to be cautious of the fact that some of our own actions could cause others to be offended, and if so, change them. Don't do those things that you know are offensive and insulting to others. Be aware of what you say. Think before you speak. Your words can destroy a person's self-esteem or they can bring them up to a higher level.

> *I THEREFORE, the prisoner for the Lord, appeal to and beg you to walk (lead a life) worthy of the*

[divine] calling to which you have been called [with behavior that is a credit to the summons to God's service,

Living as becomes you] with complete lowliness of mind (humility) and meekness (unselfishness, gentleness, mildness), with patience, bearing with one another and making allowances because you love one another.

Be eager and strive earnestly to guard and keep the harmony and oneness of [and produced by] the Spirit in the binding power of peace.

Ephesians 4:1-3
The Amplified Bible

As I mentioned before, the closer you are to a person, the more hurtful an offense can be. And Satan knows that. If you've been divorced and you're not healed of all the hurts and wounds from your first marriage, it is almost inevitable that you will carry those hurts into the second marriage and end up destroying it. It is extremely difficult to have healthy relationships when you continue to carry around all the hurts from the past. The Word of God can change that!

> *Great peace have they who love Your law; nothing shall offend them or make them stumble.*

> Psalm 119:165
> *The Amplified Bible*

You may want to write that scripture in the back of your Bible and look at it from time to time. Begin confessing: "I love God's Word above my feelings. I love God's Word above making myself feel satisfied at holding a grudge against someone who hurt me. I love God's Word, and because I love His law I'm going to have great peace in my life. I'm not going to allow anything to cause me to stumble."

How will you respond when offenses come? Don't get offended! Don't take the bait. Don't get caught in the trap. Refuse it. Forgive, forget it, and move on with God. The choice is yours.

What is your choice? God wants you to be free of offenses. Jesus said, "I am come to set the captives free." I want you to pray a prayer, and if there is something in your heart that you've been holding on to, possibly for many years, then as an act of your will, let it go today! Determine that today is your day of deliverance. You are going to feel as though a heavy, tremendous burden has been lifted from you. Are you ready? Pray this prayer and get on your way to freedom.

"Father, in the Name of Jesus, I have seen in Your Word, that I have to let offenses go. Your Word says that I must forgive those who have hurt me because You forgave me. I repent of this and I ask for Your forgiveness. I cannot forgive them in my own strength. I have to have You. Therefore, as an act of my will, I choose to forgive.

As the Heavenly Father has freely forgiven me of my sin, I freely forgive (say his/her name) for the injustice I feel they've done unto me. I forgive them. I release them. I let it go. The debt has been paid in Jesus' Name. According to Your Word, I believe that the original unpayable debt against me has been paid. I'm free! I'm free! I declare that I am free in Jesus' Name! Amen."

You are free. There's nothing holding you back. Now, be the success that God has planned for you to be.

FOR THOSE WHO DON'T KNOW JESUS, WOULD YOU LIKE TO KNOW HIM?

If you were to die today, where would you spend eternity? If you have accepted Jesus Christ as your personal Lord and Savior, you can be assured that when you die, you will go directly into the presence of God in Heaven. If you have not accepted Jesus as your personal Lord and Savior, is there any reason why you can't make Jesus the Lord of your life right now? Please pray this prayer out loud, and as you do, pray with a sincere and trusting heart, and you will be born again.

Dear God in Heaven,

I come to You in the Name of Jesus to receive salvation and eternal life. I believe that Jesus is Your Son. I believe that He died on the cross for my sins, and that You raised Him from the dead. I receive Jesus now into my heart and make Him the Lord of my life. Jesus, come into my heart. I welcome You as my Lord and Savior. Father, I believe Your Word that says I am now saved. I confess with my mouth that I am saved and born again. I am now a child of God.

JSMI

Bible Institute & School Of World Evangelism

Dear Friend,

Carolyn and I count it an honor to be involved in raising up students who will preach the uncompromised Word of God to the nations of the world. JSMI Bible Institute and School of World Evangelism is the fulfillment of a dream that was birthed in my spirit many years ago, and I am extremely excited about the potential we now have to train up students in an atmosphere charged with faith!

Our desire is to see each student develop a passion for God and a passion for souls. We endeavor to impart into each student the spirit of revival and help them become equipped and ready to participate in the last days move of God, bringing multitudes into His Kingdom.

If you are looking for a unique opportunity to increase your knowledge of the scriptures and find your place in God's plan, I trust you will prayerfully consider our school.

Sincerely,

Dr. Jerry Savelle

APPLICATION
REQUEST FORM

*Please send me an application for JSMI Bible
Institute and School Of World Evangelism*

Name _____

Address _____

City/State _____

Zip/Telephone _____

*To receive an application packet, please
complete this form, tear it out and mail today.*

**Jerry Savelle Ministries International
Bible Institute and School
of World Evangelism
P.O. Box 999
Crowley, TX 76036
817/297-2243 M-F 8:30-5:00 (CST)**

Audio Tapes by Carolyn Savelle
· How To Excel As A Woman Of God
· The Peace Of God
· God Is Light
· Inspiring Messages - Vol. 1
· Inspiring Messages - Vol. 2
· The Faith That Pleases God
· The Joy Of The Second Half Of Life
· The Fire Of God
· The Faith Of One In A Million - Joshua
And Caleb Had It And You Can Have It Too!
· What Time Is It On God's Timetable?
· How To Develop A Relationship
Between You And God
· Praying God's Will For Your Life
· How To Change Your
Circumstances Through Prayer
· Conquering The Spirit of Offense
· A Revelation Of The Blood

Single Tapes by Carolyn Savelle
· Hope: The Anchor Of Your Soul
· Thinking On The Lord
· The Heartbeat Of God Is Souls
· Born To Be A Blessing
· Overcoming Being Overwhelmed

Mini-Book by Carolyn Savelle
· Born To Be A Blessing

*For a complete list of tapes, videos and books by
Carolyn Savelle, write or call:*

**Jerry Savelle Ministries International
PO Box 748
Crowley, TX 76036
(817) 297-3155**

*Feel free to include your prayer requests
and comments when you write.*